- ENDORSEMENTS -

"Julie Ann Sullivan has nailed the essence of engagement in her book, Blueprint for Employee Engagement – 37 Essential Elements to Influence, Innovate & Inspire. A must read for any manager or leader looking to boost their own engagement or the engagement of their teams! An encyclopedia of pragmatic takeaways!"

BOB KELLEHER, AUTHOR OF *LOUDER THAN WORDS*, *10 EMPLOYEE ENGAGEMENT STEPS THAT DRIVE RESULTS* AND *EMPLOYEE ENGAGEMENT FOR DUMMIES*

"I got a million-dollar idea just from the first 3 tips!! Julie Ann Sullivan gives leaders the roadmap for changing cultures and inspiring teams to act! Well done!"

JEFFREY HAYZLETT - PRIMETIME TV & RADIO HOST, SPEAKER, AUTHOR AND PART-TIME COWBOY

"Julie Ann Sullivan's book gives you a clear understanding of an organization's foundational principles."

TOM ZIGLAR, CEO, ZIGLAR, INC. AND PROUD SON OF ZIG ZIGLAR

"Julie Ann Sullivan has laid out a great set of ways to Influence, Innovate and Inspire your teams. Culture is not part of the game, it is the game. Teach your teams how to be great by using this book as a guide for you to move from good to great and from great to greater. It is never too late to get better."

LEE COCKERELL, EXECUTIVE VICE PRESIDENT (RETIRED AND INSPIRED) WALT DISNEY WORLD® RESORT AND AUTHOR OF *CREATING MAGIC*, *THE CUSTOMER RULES*, *TIME MANAGEMENT MAGIC* AND *CAREER MAGIC.*

"Julie Ann has gathered great wisdom into easily digestible bites. Read this book to be reminded of the important things you might have forgotten and learn new ideas that will make you better."

MARK SANBORN, CSP, CPAE, SPEAKER AND AUTHOR OF *THE POTENTIAL PRINCIPLE* AND *THE FRED FACTOR*

"If you are serious about building a fast-growing company that lasts, you are at the right starting point by reading Blueprint for Employee Engagement. *It has been proven that with the right culture a company can thrive. Julie Ann is a master at telling you and showing you as a leader how to do it!"*

TANA GREENE, CEO, THE GREENE GROUP

"Julie Ann Sullivan gives us powerful, actionable ideas that can have an immediate and positive impact on creating engagement. Great tips from cover to cover!"

JOE CALLOWAY - AUTHOR - *BE THE BEST AT WHAT MATTERS MOST*

"Julie Ann is an expert in promoting positive business culture, and this book is an essential read for anyone who wants a healthier, more engaged workplace."

JASON FORREST - CEO OF FPG | HUMAN PERFORMANCE UNLEASHED

"I have read hundreds of books, interviewed hundreds of the best and the brightest business people in America, listened to and watched hundreds of podcasts and videos on leadership. So when I learn something new from an author, I'm impressed. Julie Ann Sullivan impressed me by giving me new ideas and strategies to use in my own businesses and to share with my clients. Great read, great new ways to help me 'Influence, Innovate, Inspire.'"

**MARTY WOLFF, EXECUTIVE COACH,
BUSINESS CONSULTANT, BUSINESS JOURNALIST**

"Julie Ann Sullivan takes a complex idea and breaks it into valuable tips. Each one is a golden nugget to grow your culture into a place where people want to come to work and influence the outcomes."

DR. NIDO QUBEIN – PRESIDENT, HIGH POINT UNIVERSITY

"As the guy who wrote the book on engagement, I can tell you that leaders often make it far harder and more complicated than it needs to be. A massive shift in engagement can come from consistently doing one right thing at a time. If you are looking for the one 'right thing' to do, look no further, because Julie Ann has found the 37 DNA strands of Engagement."

DOV BARON, AUTHOR OF *FIERCELY LOYAL: HOW HIGH PERFORMING COMPANIES DEVELOP AND RETAIN TOP TALENT;* **INC MAGAZINE TOP 100 LEADERSHIP SPEAKER TO HIRE**

Blueprint for Employee Engagement:
37 Essential Elements to Influence, Innovate & Inspire
By Julie Ann Sullivan

© 2017 Julie Ann Sullivan. All Rights Reserved.

Published by LNE Press

ISBN: 978-0-692-98212-9
Library of Congress Control Number: 2017917740

Cover and Book Design: Mike Murray, pearhouse.com

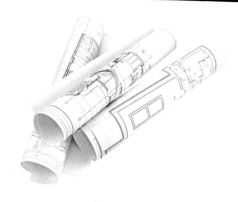

If you're a leader who wants a successful, prosperous business with a flourishing, loyal workforce, then this book is for you: 37 concepts to put into practice, one great idea at a time. Take the challenge to Influence, Innovate, and Inspire every aspect of your organization.

Ask me how we can achieve this goal together:

Julie Ann Sullivan
724-942-0486
JulieAnnSullivan.com
JulieAnn@JulieAnnSullivan.com

BLUEPRINT FOR EMPLOYEE ENGAGEMENT

37 Essential Elements to Influence, Innovate & Inspire

JULIE ANN SULLIVAN

JULIE ANN SULLIVAN

- ABOUT THE AUTHOR -

Julie Ann Sullivan works with organizations that want to create a workplace where people are productive, engaged, and appreciated. Julie Ann is a communication specialist, collaboration strategist, and change steward who brings a more positive environment to every organization she works with. She founded Learning Never Ends, a company whose purpose is to create a more positive culture, one person at a time.

Julie Ann earned a BA in psychology and an MBA in accounting. As a CPA, she spent decades in the financial industry and the corporate world. As a professional speaker, she has worked with McDonald's USA, Howard Hanna Financial, Highmark, and Bayer US.

Her programs are engaging events known for their innovation, humor, and expertise. Julie Ann is a professional member of the National Speakers Association, an accomplished author, and the host of the podcasts Mere Mortals Unite and Businesses that Care.

Contact Julie Ann to create a workplace where people are creative, productive, and loyal:

PHONE: (724) 942-0486
EMAIL: JulieAnn@JulieAnnSullivan.com
WEB: JulieAnnSullivan.com

- ACKNOWLEDGMENTS -

I wouldn't even be writing this without my Publishing Divas: Kathleen Caldwell and Sheila Anderson. Their continuous support and accountability were the cornerstone of this project. We are three very different women, coming together to learn from each other. I grew as a person as well. I love you two. Thank you to Jeffrey Hayzlett and the C-Suite Network family who game me this opportunity to step into. A shout out to Phil M. Jones, master of encouragement who moved the Divas to commitment. Thank you, Mike Murray, my friend and graphic designer, for doing everything I didn't want to do. I am always grateful for my friendship with Marylu Zuk and her willingness to take a final look at the book with her keen eye and sense of perspective. Thank you to my friends and family who encourage me every day, especially the Power Women of the National Speakers Association and my neighbors, Nick and Kristen Goodell.

Last but not least I want to say thank you to all the businesses I have worked with, especially those that have shared their true spirit of employee engagement on the Businesses that Care podcast. You continue to inspire me.

- CONTENTS -

About the Author i

Acknowledgments iii

Introduction:
Why Should You Care? 3

How It Works 7

#1 Accountability 8

#2 Attention 10

#3 Attitude 12

#4 Authenticity 14

#5 Celebration 16

#6 Choice 18

#7 Clarity 20

#8 Collaboration 22

#9 Communication 24

#10 Community 26

#11 Compliment 28

#12 Creativity 30

#13 Curiosity 32

#14 Disengagement 34

#15 Empowerment 36

#16 Encouragement 38

#17 Flexibility 40

#18 Focus 42

#19 Forgiveness 44

#20 Fun 46

#21 Gratitude 48

#22 Inclusivity 50

#23 Judgment 52

#24 Leadership 54

#25 Modeling 56

#26 Patience 58

#27 Perspective 60

#28 Purpose 62

#29 Recognition 64

#30 Reinforcement 66

#31 Relationships 68

#32 Resilience 70

#33 Respect 72

#34 Self-awareness 74

#35 Service 76

#36 Simplify 78

#37 Trust 80

What Do You Do Now? 83

- INTRODUCTION -

WHY SHOULD YOU CARE?

Nearly two-thirds of American workers are disengaged at some level. The resulting loss of productivity costs companies over $500 billion every year. How much of that belongs to you? By some estimates, an increase of just 5% in productivity in a company with 50 employees could reap $150,000 more in profit.

A labor shortage has already begun and will get larger. We are reaching a tipping point. Those who don't start now will not have enough workforce to deliver their company's goods and services—all the more reason to start and expand employee engagement practices.

The words "employee engagement" have been so overused that some leaders have become desensitized to the concept and its benefits. Don't be numbed by the overabundance of articles, apps, and services in this space. If you're a leader who wants a successful, prosperous business with a flourishing, loyal workforce, then this book is for you: 37 concepts to put into practice, one great idea at a time. Take the challenge to Influence, Innovate, and Inspire every aspect of your organization.

Influence is what you have only when people are open to accepting it. The best way to influence those around you is to act how you want them to act. Your organization will Innovate when its creativity and problem solving are improved by the ideas in this book. And, the greatest gift you can give is to Inspire your people to act in a way that is beyond the potential they saw in themselves.

This book is anchored in research. Over the past decade, we've seen a plethora of studies on the correlation between happier, engaged people and their level of success in their relationships at home and in the workplace. Like it or not, happier people create better teams. Would you be interested in lower absenteeism, fewer mistakes, greater loyalty, and higher productivity?

Start with one tip and build it into the fabric of your culture. You can't know if something works if you don't use it. Make your trial period long enough to really test if a new idea is working. It may take a month, six months, or a year—but it won't be tomorrow. Evaluate the results, make adjustments, and retain what works best for you and your organization.

Every idea in this book can be learned and become a habit with strategic repetition and reinforcement. They are simple, but not easy. You need to make consistent, deliberate choices each day to master these elements and carry them into the future. You will also notice many of these ideas are interrelated. For example, how can you have accountability without trust? The relationships between such concepts are complex, but this book breaks them down into individual tips, where each one is attainable and can be put to work to create a culture filled with engagement and success.

Remember: these are concepts, not total solutions, essences, not thorough philosophies. I could talk for hours about any of these ideas, with real-life examples to show you how they breed success. For now, I want to start the conversation by making you aware of the importance of each concept to your organizational growth. I want you to take away helpful ideas you can implement immediately.

This is the first step in creating a culture of engagement. These are not all the steps that can make a positive difference in your business. For each element you master and create space for in your workplace culture, every aspect of your business will grow. This is true from the front line, to the C-Suite, to your customers. Are you up for the challenge?

- HOW IT WORKS -

Each chapter gives you an easy visual
guide to get what you need:

The definition.

The answer to the most important question:
What's in it for me?

An action to take now.

Are you ready to grow?

#1

ACCOUNTABILITY

AN OBLIGATION OR WILLINGNESS TO
ACCEPT RESPONSIBILITY FOR ONE'S ACTIONS.

Without accountability, you would live and work in a world without confidence. It would be almost impossible to plan a day if you had no reasonable confidence that, at the very least, people would show up and complete their tasks. Envision a workplace where no one did what they said they would do. A place where no one felt responsible for themselves or their team. Is that where you want to work?

If you want people around you to be accountable, then you must do what you say, too. You don't live in a vacuum; you work with a team. Following through on your own obligations creates a better work environment for all the stakeholders. Take 10% of the time that you worry about others doing their job and concentrate on yourself. Replace blame with understanding how you may have created a situation that went awry. Make sure you are setting an example that you want to be followed.

What do you need to do to ensure that your culture breeds accountability and removes the fear of admitting when errors are made?

"IT IS NOT ONLY WHAT WE DO,
BUT ALSO WHAT WE
DO NOT DO FOR WHICH
WE ARE ACCOUNTABLE."

– JOHN-BAPTISTE MOLIÈRE –

#2

ATTENTION

THE ACT OF APPLYING THE MIND TO SOMETHING.

The simple act of paying attention creates higher quality work, whether in services or products. Having fewer failures, errors, quality defects, and accidents leads to an increase in the bottom line and the overall morale of a workplace environment. On an interpersonal level, truly paying attention to a colleague creates a bond that transcends every interaction you have together. In a world where we see millions of bits of information every day, paying attention has become a skill that needs to be reintroduced and retooled.

Pay more attention to what is going on around you. Create space in your day to notice a colleague doing something well. Acknowledge what you observe directly to them and explain exactly what they did. Instead of a nondescript "Good job," be specific: "You handled the interaction with Mr. Smith well."

How many times a day do you stop to notice what those around you are doing? How often do you express an encouraging word?

"THE QUALITY OF YOUR LIFE IS DETERMINED BY THE FOCUS OF YOUR ATTENTION."

– CHERI HUBER –

#3

ATTITUDE

A MENTAL POSITION ABOUT A FACT OR SITUATION.

Viktor Frankl survived a concentration camp by understanding his attitude was the one aspect of his life he could control. Attitude is an important piece of your life that you may not even think about. Not thinking about it creates the inability to control it. When you realize the control you have over your attitude, you create a crucial difference in how you cope with everything that happens. Your destiny can change.

The next time you have the opportunity to recognize an experience in your day that is different than what you had planned, notice how you react. You can only change or celebrate what you notice. Then, take 10 seconds to find an alternative way to see the situation. Finally, think about what have you learned.

How would your work environment be different if you decided to see an opportunity where you would normally see an annoyance? What would happen if you chose to have a different perspective?

"EVERYTHING CAN BE TAKEN FROM A MAN BUT ONE THING: THE LAST OF HUMAN FREEDOMS—TO CHOOSE ONE'S ATTITUDE IN ANY GIVEN SET OF CIRCUMSTANCES, TO CHOOSE ONE'S OWN WAY."

– VIKTOR FRANKL –

#4

AUTHENTICITY

BEING TRUE TO ONE'S OWN PERSONALITY, SPIRIT OR CHARACTER.

It can be a little scary to be who you truly are, but it is your most successful self. Pushing yourself into a mold that doesn't fit is painful and self-defeating. It requires work to take a deep look inward and find out who you are. Have the courage to be that person in all you do. That doesn't mean you do not change and grow. Being a lifelong learner is a great character strength. The outcome will be that those around you can count on who you are and rely on your honesty. This quality is essential in great leaders. Companies are also subject to scrutiny of their authenticity. To have an engaged workplace, a company must act like the values it incorporates in its mission and value statements.

Check often to see if you're true to yourself and your company's vision. Make the necessary adjustments. If you want integrity, you can't be involved with unscrupulous practices. Employees are smart. They look for you to walk your talk. Review what you ask from your workforce and then analyze your business practices. Are they in alignment with one another?

How would your day be different if you thought about how each action aligns with your vision and mission?

"PERFECTION IS THE ENEMY OF AUTHENTICITY."

– LISA BRAITHWAITE –

#5

CELEBRATION

TO MARK SOMETHING (SUCH AS AN ANNIVERSARY) BY
FESTIVITIES OR OTHER DEVIATION FROM THE ROUTINE.

A job well-done, whether a phone conversation or a completed project, deserves recognition. Being recognized is one of the top 10 benefits people look for in job satisfaction. Many companies mistakenly wait until a two-year project is complete, or get stuck on the idea that a celebration needs to be a planned event. But the definition of celebration includes a deviation from the routine. That's all it needs to be. Celebrating accomplishment, especially a small victory, creates a more uplifting spirit in your environment so productivity and innovation will flourish.

Why wait? Encourage celebration. Ask your employees to find reasons to celebrate. Create a calendar that celebrates teddy bear day, Hawaiian shirt day, or sandwich day. Create a rotating committee to choose the ideas and how to celebrate them. Change your mindset to one that searches for reasons to say, "Good job."

What do you think your work environment would feel like if the focus of the day was to notice an act of kindness and acknowledge it?

"UNTIL FURTHER NOTICE,
CELEBRATE EVERYTHING."

– UNKNOWN –

#6

CHOICE

CARE IN SELECTING.

When fear and anxiety take over, it becomes difficult to perceive alternatives. Sometimes we don't see other possibilities because we don't like them, so we act like they don't exist. There is hope to overcome this. When you deliberately choose to look for more than one path, more paths appear. Then you have an opportunity to compare your choice to your alternatives. Whatever alternative you choose, dig into the positive aspects, however small they may be.

Change brings excellent opportunities to learn about a different perspective. Once a change is implemented, new ideas usually come to light. When you have a new policy, procedure, boss, location, or customer, think about all the choices you make to deal with that situation. Go beyond your original thought, and you will easily create a path to success.

Imagine no choice and then search for more choices than you originally thought of. When you act in this way, what changes in your perspective?

"LIFE IS A MATTER OF CHOICES,
AND EVERY CHOICE
YOU MAKE
MAKES YOU."

– JOHN C. MAXWELL –

#7

CLARITY

THE QUALITY OF BEING EASILY UNDERSTOOD.

This skill is the difference between being understood or confused. It works whether you are giving information or receiving it. As the speaker, clarity ensures your instructions are understood and translated into action, therefore saving precious time. So much time is lost because questions of a defining nature have yet to be asked. If you are the listener, it's your responsibility to understand what is being asked of you. If you don't comprehend the message, you need to ask for clarification. Sooner is more efficient than later.

The next time a colleague asks you for clarification, think about how you could have written or spoken the instructions in the first place so they would have made more sense. This exercise is less frustrating when you accept that everyone learns differently. What might seem like too much work and time at the start, can be a conduit for a quicker and higher quality result. Think of your goal and how best to reach it. It's worth the effort.

What can you do to be more specific about your needs and the goals of your company?

"A LACK OF CLARITY COULD
PUT THE BRAKES ON ANY
JOURNEY TO SUCCESS."

– STEVE MARABOLI –

#8

COLLABORATION

TO WORK JOINTLY WITH OTHERS, ESPECIALLY IN AN INTELLECTUAL ENDEAVOR.

Individuals who successfully work with others transform a work environment from stressful and uninspiring to engaging and uplifting. Learning to not take things personally, and understanding the power of acceptance, allows a team to focus on getting results. With self-exploration and effective collaborative skills, all team members have an opportunity for improved interaction and achievement. The ability to accept differences in others is directly proportional to how productive a team can be. All businesses and organizations are teams. Inspired teamwork and collaboration creates a cohesive and successful workplace culture.

Make sure your teams have the skills to work together beyond their area of expertise. Give them training on how to work together effectively on any project, not just the project at hand. Have them find what commonalities they have with one another beyond work. This builds cohesiveness. Simple, low-cost exercises can accomplish this. The cost is well worth the increased productivity and innovation, and the improved problem solving.

Picture your workplace with fewer interpersonal conflicts and inconveniences. What more could you achieve?

"GREAT THINGS IN BUSINESS
ARE NEVER DONE BY ONE
PERSON; THEY'RE DONE
BY A TEAM OF PEOPLE."

– STEVE JOBS –

#9

COMMUNICATION

A PROCESS BY WHICH INFORMATION IS EXCHANGED BETWEEN INDIVIDUALS THROUGH A COMMON SYSTEM OF SYMBOLS, SIGNS, OR BEHAVIOR.

Success does not exist without good communication. Whether you are a CEO talking to your workforce, or a salesperson speaking with your customers, communication is the cornerstone of relationship building. If you can't talk to someone, you certainly can't work well together. There are two sides to communication: sender and receiver. Both have their unique responsibilities. Learn how to convey your message well and become accomplished in the art of listening. These are strategic skills for success.

Remember when you were a kid and you were taught to think before you speak? The next time you have a conversation, keep in mind the following:

- Who are you talking to?
- What is the goal of the conversation?
- Are you in the right location and frame of mind to have this exchange?
- Have you had enough time to think about it beforehand to make it meaningful?

Attention to these objectives will create efficient and effective communication.

Notice what happens when you listen without always thinking about what you want to say next.

"WE HAVE TWO EARS AND ONE MOUTH SO THAT WE CAN LISTEN TWICE AS MUCH AS WE SPEAK."

– EPICTETUS –

#10

COMMUNITY

AN INTERACTING POPULATION OF VARIOUS INDIVIDUALS IN A COMMON LOCATION.

Humans have craved a sense of belonging ever since they lived in caves. Being welcoming and willing to share are fundamental requirements for a well-functioning group. Extreme competition in the workplace can actually stifle sales and cause underperformance in customer service. But when the working environment includes the sharing of ideas and best practices, then sales, productivity, and customer retention increase. The idea that you are there to help one another boosts the power to exceed expectations. Customers feel like they have a "village" to service them. A mutually supportive group worries less about its future when one person leaves the organization.

Bring your sales teams together to discuss what is working for them and what isn't. In each department, use real-life issues to think as a group about how to deal with those situations in an efficiently and effectively. This sharing of ideas will create a collective of better problem solvers. It's easy to work under perfect conditions; but when snags happen, people need to know who to turn to.

How different would your bottom-line results be if people worked with each other instead of against each other?

"ONLY IN COMMUNITY DO
WE HAVE THE RESOURCES TO
HELP EVERYONE SUCCEED."
– JULIE ANN SULLIVAN –

#11

COMPLIMENT

AN EXPRESSION OF ESTEEM, RESPECT,
AFFECTION, OR ADMIRATION.

Here is an easy tip to build a culture of engagement. It costs nothing, takes little time, and makes a positive difference for everyone involved. Have you ever walked into work feeling bad, and someone gave you a compliment? Even if just for a moment, you felt better, lighter, and happier—right? If so, then you know how a compliment can make a person feel. I always wonder why then we don't take the time to share them.

Next time you're thinking a kind thought about someone, share it. Check out the person's face. I'll bet you see at least traces of a smile. When you receive a compliment, let it soak in. Say, "Thank you," and then say no more. If you negate it in any way, it's as if you are refusing a gift. And no one wants to hear a long story about what you just got complimented on either. You might find that last part takes some practice.

How could you change the human environment around you by giving compliments? What would that feel like to you, to make that difference in someone else's life?

"A COMPLIMENT IS
VERBAL SUNSHINE."

– ROBERT ORBEN –

#12

CREATIVITY

THE ABILITY TO MAKE NEW THINGS OR THINK OF NEW IDEAS.

Without new ideas, your business would be stagnant. You would eventually be overtaken by competitors who are not afraid to try a new direction. I am not advocating running after whatever seems cool at the moment. Instead, a well thought out vision can turn a mediocre company into a thriving one. Our world is changing faster every moment. If you understand and accept from the outset that some ideas will work and some won't, then you will have less reluctance to seek ingenuity and innovation.

Don't let fear stop you from prospering from a new idea. From offices to factories, creativity can create a renewed sense of empowerment. You might create a reward program for workers who come up with new ideas to streamline a process. On a regular basis, include in your collaborative meetings a discussion about what isn't working. Continue by discussing ideas on how to ensure those predicaments don't happen again. Your people best understand the situations they confront every day; the more you involve them in generating a solution, the more they will buy into it, use it, and feel comfortable doing so.

What area of your company will innovation improve? What's stopping you?

"THERE IS NO INNOVATION
AND CREATIVITY WITHOUT
FAILURE. PERIOD."

– **BRENÉ BROWN** –

#13

CURIOSITY

THE DESIRE TO KNOW.

To have innovation flourish, allow your workforce to be curious. If you allow the status quo to be your standard, then you will never grow—and neither will your business. The expansion of your vision, for your organization or yourself, starts with wondering, "What would happen if…" People need to feel they work in an environment where they can ask questions. Giving them permission to explore will create an atmosphere where people and ideas blossom. Great leaders design a world where individuals that want to grow, can.

The next time you have a team meeting, ask, "What if?" Purposely think of different ways to do your current processes. Even if you only find out why alternatives won't work, this process will help everyone use their brain for exploring and problem solving. You want a team of people who can think when life throws them a curve ball. This type of training will give them confidence in their abilities.

What barriers would be quashed if you took the time to inquire?

"I DON'T KNOW WHAT
I DON'T KNOW."

– JEFFREY HAYZLETT –

#14

DISENGAGEMENT

THE STATE OF BEING RELEASED OR DETACHED FROM SOMETHING.

In a world where more than 200 million emails are sent each day, it's no wonder there seems to be no time to relax. You need to make the time. Disengaging is a necessity for mental and physical well-being. Your health directly effects every aspect of your work. Managing stress involves awareness and the willingness to take action. Finding calm increases focus, productivity, and good health.

Research-based techniques for strategic disengagement are simple. Start small, but be deliberate. Concentrate on your breathing for 30 seconds. Slowly inhale and exhale. After a week, increase to a minute. See if you can build up to breathing for two minutes. Don't you deserve that amount of time each day? Recognize your own behaviors. When you feel tense, counteract it with something that makes you feel relaxed. Step outside, drink a glass of water, listen to some music, or watch a funny video. Choose what works for you, but take action.

The next time you get annoyed, how would pausing in the moment change your outlook?

"THE TIME TO RELAX
IS WHEN YOU DON'T
HAVE THE TIME FOR IT."
– SIDNEY J. HARRIS –

#15

EMPOWERMENT

TO PROMOTE THE SELF-ACTUALIZATION OR INFLUENCE OF SOMEONE.

This concept is mastered when you allow people to be the best they can be. With empowerment, productivity and innovation can grow tenfold. As a leader, allowing people to expand their capabilities can be difficult. The unknown is risky for results minded people. What you might discover are new strengths in your workforce. Great leaders delegate and give team members an opportunity to expand their potential.

The next time someone on your team expresses a problem, ask them if they can come up with some solutions. Giving an individual the support to solve a situation increases their value. Their idea may stink, or they may realize the status quo is the best solution, or they may come up with a great new idea. Either way, you have encouraged them to flourish. Micromanaging, on the other hand, kills growth.

How can you foster in others a feeling of having permission to flourish?

"PEOPLE WANT GUIDANCE, NOT RHETORIC. THEY NEED TO KNOW WHAT THE PLAN OF ACTION IS AND HOW IT WILL BE IMPLEMENTED. THEY WANT TO BE GIVEN RESPONSIBILITY TO HELP SOLVE THE PROBLEM AND THE AUTHORITY TO ACT ON IT."

– HOWARD SCHULTZ –

#16

ENCOURAGEMENT

THE ACT OF MAKING SOMETHING MORE
APPEALING OR MORE LIKELY TO HAPPEN.

Inspiration. Praise. Boosting esteem. Each of these can be an avenue for instilling the vision of possibilities. Everyone likes to know they have value. Encouragement is a way to communicate that you believe another can do what they set out to do. On the receiving end, feeling like someone "has your back" may be just the support someone needs to keep moving forward. Work can be frustrating, but a little bit of support can go a long way in alleviating that.

If you really want to spread encouragement like a wildfire in your culture, build it into the fabric of everything you do. I worked with a brake company whose tag line was We Save Lives. They used it everywhere: check stubs, posters, newsletters, offices, break rooms, and parties. Place encouraging words for every department and job type to see. While encouraging support, you build community, too.

How would morale change if there were uplifting messages everywhere you turn?

"NOTHING IS IMPOSSIBLE,
THE WORD ITSELF
SAYS I'M POSSIBLE."

– AUDREY HEPBURN –

#17

FLEXIBILITY

ADAPTABILITY TO NEW, DIFFERENT, OR CHANGING REQUIREMENTS.

In today's quickly changing world, the ability to think and act differently is essential. This can be applied to your personal and professional life. Have you ever had a day completely go according to plan? Probably not. Flexibility is essential for the presence of mind you need to work and live a successful life. People who are more adaptable to change can move beyond the glitches life serves up daily. Teaching flexibility will reduce the amount of stress inside your workplace and out. There really is no separating the two.

Flexibility can be of the mind or body. Accept that each individual is unique in your workforce. Take the initiative to communicate through different means, whether auditory, visual or some combination of both. Your message needs to be delivered to ensure that everyone gets the same meaning. Environments that instill innovation need to be flexible too. Create an area where folks can gather informally to collaborate, instead of signing up for the conference room next week at 11:15 for 45 minutes. Rigidity is not conducive to spontaneous, creative though.

What can you gain from trying something new?

"STAY COMMITTED TO YOUR DECISIONS, BUT STAY FLEXIBLE IN YOUR APPROACH."

– TONY ROBBINS –

#18

FOCUS

A STATE OF CLEAR PERCEPTION OR UNDERSTANDING.

Focusing on multitasking is an oxymoron. You can do more than one activity at a time, but you can't do them well. Train your brain to focus on what is right in front of you. You can teach your brain not to wander. I'm a "squirrel" kind of woman, so I know how difficult this can be. It's worth the effort. When you focus on each moment in time, you have a much clearer sense of purpose. This ability allows you to use your experience and expertise for maximum performance. Learning to focus increases the value of your time spent, therefore adding to your efficiency. You can gain time—and who doesn't want that.

Make it a goal in your next meeting to stay focused. Go in with a specific objective and scrupulously keep to it. If everyone is informed at the outset, then when your singular purpose is implemented, everyone in the room will be on board. This takes practice, but you'll be amazed at how much shorter and productive your meetings become.

Where else in your life could being focused work to your advantage?

"STARVE YOUR DISTRACTIONS, FEED YOUR FOCUS."

– UNKNOWN –

#19

FORGIVENESS

ALLOWING ROOM FOR ERROR OR WEAKNESS.

No one is perfect. People make mistakes. You make mistakes. The words "I'm sorry" are life-altering. Forgiveness is a part of the process of letting go. It's about acceptance, not agreement. Since there is no way yet to go back in time and change your actions, one alternative is to carry regrets and personal baggage around. That pent-up negativity can adversely affect your health, both physically and emotionally. Your success depends on you finding another way.

Try these alternatives instead of carrying around angst and anger. If you forgot to do something, maybe you could develop a checklist. If you barked at someone because you were running late, apologize. If someone else acted in a way that bothers you, maybe they're not a person you want to be involved with. If you must be involved with them, set strict boundaries. If boundaries are unworkable, maybe it's time to move on.

How could a relationship grow if you were willing to apologize or accept an apology?

"HOLDING A GRUDGE DOESN'T MAKE YOU STRONG; IT MAKES YOU BITTER. FORGIVING DOESN'T MAKE YOU WEAK; IT SETS YOU FREE."

– DAVE WILLIS –

#20

FUN

A MOOD FOR FINDING OR MAKING AMUSEMENT.

Everyone wants to have fun, but for too long you've been taught that having a good time is incongruous with working hard. A manager once told me I was obviously not working hard enough because I had too good of an attitude. That relationship didn't last. In a company where people have fun together, people create new ideas and solve problems better. Finding the fun in a project alleviates stress and creates an atmosphere for higher quality work.

Engage your workforce by creating a culture council or a fun squad. Have them suggest ideas on how to take a break from too much thinking or too much staring at screens. Create a fun room where people can take a break. Fill it with games, bubbles, funny magazines, and videos. There are endless ways to stimulate people's funny bones. Even celebrating birthdays, newborns, or new puppies is a way to have fun. Get creative.

What would it be like to work in a place where fun was planned?

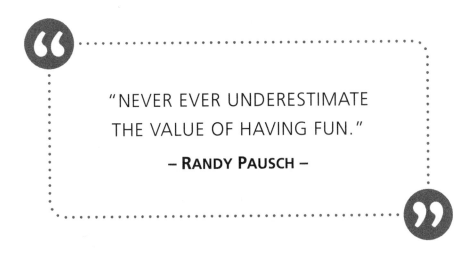

"NEVER EVER UNDERESTIMATE
THE VALUE OF HAVING FUN."
– RANDY PAUSCH –

#21

GRATITUDE

A FEELING OF APPRECIATION OR THANKS.

For more than a decade, researchers have been studying the effects of a positive mindset and its byproducts of increased productivity, creativity, and engagement. Gratitude creates this optimistic way of thinking. Grateful people can have 10% fewer stress-related illnesses, be better problem solvers, have higher quality work and less frequent absenteeism. This is how gratitude shows up in the bottom line of any business.

There is great power in these two words: "Thank you." When you say that directly and are specific on what you noticed that made a difference, a relationship grows. These days, every aspect of a business is about relationships. Instead of walking by and saying, "Thanks," use something like this: "Thank you, Sam, for taking the time to call the Jones Company to make sure they got our product. It makes a difference." Specificity creates additional value.

What would happen to your mindset if every day you searched for something new to be grateful for?

"YOU CAN'T WALK IN
GRATITUDE AND SIT IN
SELF-PITY AT THE SAME TIME."

– MARILYN SHERMAN –

#22

INCLUSIVITY

COVERING OR INCLUDING EVERYTHING.

This idea goes way beyond diversity. It means constantly finding ways to include and engage everyone in your workforce. A great workplace starts with people who feel like they belong. You create that inclusive atmosphere by being mindful in every aspect of your business. The results are greater loyalty, lower turnover, and a more cohesive work environment.

When creating your next project team, why not ask who would like to be a part of it? You might be surprised who will step up. Even more surprising might be hidden talents that lay dormant in a person's current position. If possible, find a place for them, no matter how small. This will instill the feelings of accomplishment and belonging. Who knows? You might be surprised to find valuable attributes that will benefit everyone.

If you discover talent that may have been overlooked, what can that add to your overall success?

"THERE IS ONLY ONE WAY TO LOOK AT THINGS UNTIL SOMEONE SHOW US HOW TO LOOK AT THEM WITH DIFFERENT EYES."

– PABLO PICASSO –

#23

JUDGMENT

FORMING AN OPINION OR EVALUATION
BY DISCERNING AND COMPARING.

In an instant, you make judgments about how someone looks, or why they act the way they do. You do it a thousand times a day, often on a subconscious level. You might not even base that opinion on any facts, only past experiences that may have nothing to do with the person at hand. The problem with this behavior is that we react and make decisions on these judgments. This can harm the way your business runs, and certainly affects your relationships.

First, you must be aware of how your brain works. You need to become more familiar with what you think, as it is happening. Only then can you stop and make another choice. In the next conversation you have, ask yourself if you are assuming the "why" behind the other person's words. The next time you are annoyed with someone's behavior, ask yourself why you are annoyed, instead of blaming them. Be transparent with yourself and be aware how often you judge without evidence.

What would happen if you were to catch yourself assuming and ask for clarification instead?

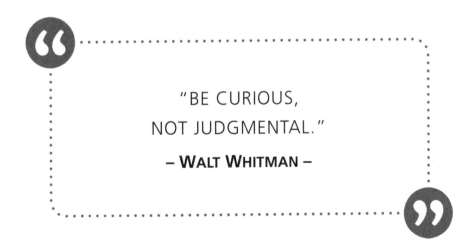

"BE CURIOUS,
NOT JUDGMENTAL."

– WALT WHITMAN –

#24

LEADERSHIP

THE CAPACITY TO LEAD.

The word "lead" is vital to the definition of leadership. If you are leading, others are following, and you must give them a reason. "Lead" is often used incorrectly as a synonym for "manage." Managing is for things. Leadership is for people. Leadership is a skill that is continually tested and refined. You are asking people to come on a ride with you. A leader explains the benefits and then makes sure they are available along the way. Great leaders empower people to become more than they thought possible.

To create great leadership, learn constantly. Learn what other successful people know by reading books and articles, or listening to podcasts to stay current. Mastermind groups are a terrific way to be with like minds with different perspectives. You could also ask the people you work with, "What is working, and what could be improved?" This vulnerability is a good quality to have.

What are you doing in your company to create an atmosphere where people want to take the ride with you?

"THE CHALLENGE OF LEADERSHIP IS TO BE STRONG, BUT NOT RUDE; BE KIND, BUT NOT WEAK; BE BOLD, BUT NOT A BULLY; BE THOUGHTFUL, BUT NOT LAZY; BE HUMBLE, BUT NOT TIMID; BE PROUD, BUT NOT ARROGANT; HAVE HUMOR, BUT WITHOUT FOLLY."

– JIM ROHN –

#25

MODELING

BEING A VERY GOOD EXAMPLE OF SOMETHING.

"**D**o as I say, not as I do" is a horrible way to teach and engage your workforce. Be mindful of the actions you take. Be aware of the way you react to a situation, and the language and body language you use. Each of these must be examples of what you are looking for in people you want to work with. Your colleagues, employees, managers, executives, and owners are watching. Success thrives in a workplace where a good attitude, peak performance, and resiliency are a part of the norm.

Ask yourself and your workforce to be accountable. Find a behavior within that you would like others to imitate. Expose it. Make that type of behavior a priority company wide. Then together, search for behaviors that need enhancing. Support one another with ideas to develop better living examples to emulate. When you have built an organization filled with trust, you can ask others to do this with you. This process further increases the connection necessary to fulfill your potential together.

Can you imagine improving a behavior that might affect an entire team? What would that be?

"DO SOMETHING WONDERFUL.
PEOPLE MAY IMITATE IT."
– ALBERT SCHWEITZER –

#26

PATIENCE

THE ABILITY TO WAIT FOR A LONG TIME WITHOUT BECOMING ANNOYED OR UPSET.

The definition says, "A long time," but that is a relative term. It will be different for each person and circumstance. We often create our own impatience. Losing patience with yourself can be cured by taking action. When you get impatient with a human or machine, it is your reaction that affects the rest of your life. Create more patience by learning the line between letting go and knowing when to step in. This is a valuable lesson that will help alleviate stress in your life.

Patience is learned, not inherent. You learn by example and experience. Work on having more patience for the circumstances that flow into your life. Recognize when they have little or no real impact in your life. This week, when you become impatient, first decide if you are in control of the situation. If not, let it go. If yes, do something that will influence the circumstance. Practice patience. Practice some more. Practice still more.

What happens to your reaction when you take the time to PAUSE?

"GOD, GRANT ME PATIENCE.
BUT HURRY."

– UNKNOWN –

#27

PERSPECTIVE

A WAY OF THINKING ABOUT AND UNDERSTANDING SOMETHING, SUCH AS AN ISSUE OR LIFE IN GENERAL.

If you see the world as black and white, right or wrong, my way or the wrong way, you are limiting your ability to be innovative, creative, and open to growth. To have a new perspective, you need to be open to another point of view. Listening is the key. There may be a piece of what you hear that can give you a broader sense of how to move forward in a situation. This is an opportunity. Take it.

At your next team meeting, make a special announcement. Ask each person during your time together, to find one new idea, process or way of approach that they would be willing to implement in their daily work. Inquire why this process might have been difficult. What was it they had to put aside to widen their original thought process? Guidance on the benefits and barriers of finding new perspectives is a gift you can give your team.

What will happen when perspectives are broadened?

"IF YOU CHANGE THE WAY YOU LOOK AT THINGS, THE THINGS YOU LOOK AT CHANGE."

– DR. WAYNE DYER –

#28

PURPOSE

AN OBJECT OR END TO BE ATTAINED.

Does your workforce know the greater purpose of your business? Do they know the difference between their purpose at work versus the purpose of their work? Do you educate them? When people have a sense of purpose, what they do daily becomes more meaningful. This intention creates greater quality in what they produce. Understanding the big "why" leads to a workforce that is reliable and goal-oriented. Extra Bonus: Studies show that a sense of purpose can add years to your life.

If you sell mortgages, filling out paperwork can be the purpose at work, but providing a home for someone can be the purpose of the work. If you manufacture brake shoes, adding a widget to the assembly can be the purpose at work, but saving lives is the purpose of the work. Remind your workforce of the purpose that makes everyone's job worth it. Market the purpose to your people like you would to your customers, so they will be aware of the larger objective.

How will you inform your workforce about the true purpose of your product or service?

"THE TWO MOST IMPORTANT DAYS IN YOUR LIFE ARE THE DAY YOU ARE BORN AND THE DAY YOU FIND OUT WHY."

– MARK TWAIN –

#29

RECOGNITION

DICTIONARY

SPECIAL NOTICE OR ATTENTION.

WIIFM

What do people really want from their jobs? Everyone wants a paycheck, but people also want to be acknowledged and feel they are valued. Research shows employee recognition is the number one driver of engagement. Employee recognition is much more than perks or gifts. It's about being present, listening, and genuinely appreciating people for who they are and what they bring to the team. Focus on connecting the dots between what they do and how that affects the entire culture.

On a regular basis, create an opportunity for the people in your organization to identify a positive action someone took. It could be finding a solution to a problem, creating a way to streamline a process, or making the first pot of coffee in the morning. Motivating this kind of behavior will generate positive synergy among colleagues. The more this behavior is encouraged, the more it will be developed on its own.

How much would your culture be enriched if you acknowledged someone for a job well-done each day?

"THERE ARE TWO THINGS
PEOPLE WANT MORE
THAN SEX AND MONEY:
RECOGNITION AND PRAISE."

– MARY KAY ASH –

#30

REINFORCEMENT

STRENGTHENING OR ENCOURAGING SOMETHING;
THE ACT OF SAYING OR DOING SOMETHING AGAIN.

If you are interested in results, then reinforcement is necessary to support new ideas. Whether you purchase a new software or change the structure of the organization, support for a new set of circumstances will ensure your people acclimate to them smoothly. For instance, if you have training on creating better communication, you want those ideas to stick; that requires reinforcing what was taught. This can be done through repetition, which strengthens the learning process. To sustain new concepts, strategically place reminders in the workplace.

Create varied ways in which you communicate with your people: emails, podcasts, posters, books, or a useful trinket. Let's say you want to reinforce safety next month. You might create a phrase like "Pay Attention" and drop it in everything that is read. If you ask your workforce to engage in creating the best way to do this, you will add another layer to your reinforcement and engagement.

What needs to be strengthened in your organization to enhance your core values?

"YOU TEACH PEOPLE HOW TO TREAT YOU BY WHAT YOU ALLOW, WHAT YOU STOP, AND WHAT YOU REINFORCE."

– TONY GASKINS –

#31

RELATIONSHIPS

HOW TWO OR MORE PEOPLE OR GROUPS TALK TO,
BEHAVE TOWARD, AND DEAL WITH EACH OTHER.

Everything in business is built on relationships. Great connections make for heightened creativity and innovation when designing new services or products. A workforce that feels like a family has higher productivity and healthier lifestyles. A salesforce sells more when it understands it serves a customer best by knowing what the customer needs. A positive rapport creates a culture where people work better together, and work better for your clients.

Thousands of activities can build better relationships. Here's one example. At your next meeting or gathering, ask people to solicit answers to specific questions. For instance: where were you born, where did you go on vacation, or what was the best movie you ever saw? These conversations develop connections that create a culture of engagement.

What new relationship will you choose to foster today?

"IF YOU BELIEVE BUSINESS
IS BUILT ON RELATIONSHIPS,
MAKE BUILDING THEM
YOUR BUSINESS."

– SCOTT STRATTEN –

#32

RESILIENCE

AN ABILITY TO RECOVER FROM OR ADJUST EASILY TO MISFORTUNE OR CHANGE.

Notice the definition says misfortune or change. Change doesn't need to be misfortune. Perceiving how change can be good builds resilience. Be more flexible than rigid. The more stringent you are in how you perceive and manage life's situations, the more stressful it is. A workforce with resilience and flexibility stands out. They will overcome obstacles more easily therefore performing at a higher level.

The next time a colleague approaches you about struggling with a situation, suggest a new perspective or a wait-and-see attitude. Too often, we involve our emotions in a crisis that hasn't really happened yet. Being more open, flexible and resilient with small variations in the status quo will be good practice for larger disruptions. It isn't a question of if they will happen; it's when. Will you be ready?

How can you demonstrate good responses to change in your existing environment?

"WHEN YOU COME TO
THE END OF YOUR ROPE,
TIE A KNOT AND HANG ON."
– FRANKLIN D. ROOSEVELT –

#33

RESPECT

ADMIRATION OF SOMEONE OR SOMETHING THAT IS GOOD, VALUABLE, OR IMPORTANT.

Respect is earned, not demanded. Relationships in the workplace thrive on respect. To be admired, do what you say you will do. One of the quickest ways to lose respect is to give a verbal promise and then act completely to the contrary. As a leader, your behavior of respecting all levels of workers will permeate throughout the organization. On the other hand, a lack of respect has expensive consequences in loss of talent and poor morale. People thrive in a workplace culture where mutual respect is fundamental to how everyone is treated.

Listening, even without agreement to what is being said, is one of the highest forms of respect. Practice catching your mind wandering while you are being spoken to. How many times are you thinking about what you want to say before those speaking have finished their thought? Is it possible you are looking around the room to see who else you might want to talk to next? Each of these instances reduces the respect for the person right in front of you. They know it. How would it make you feel?

How are you showing people in your workforce your confidence in and admiration of them?

"I WAS RAISED TO TREAT THE JANITOR WITH THE SAME RESPECT AS THE CEO."

— JANELLE MONAE —

#34

SELF-AWARENESS

A COGNIZANCE OF ONE'S OWN
PERSONALITY OR INDIVIDUALITY.

Self-awareness is the very foundation of all the other tips in this book. You can never have too much, and without it you cannot change your behavior or grow. You need to know who you are before you can move and change to a different direction. When you build a culture where people are encouraged to expand their awareness, they in turn are more mindful about everything they do. This creates a better sense of accomplishment and eagerness to take on new challenges.

Make practicing awareness a standard way of behaving in your workplace culture. Offer the opportunity for people to share an action or behavior they are proud of. For example, you could have "Bragging Rights Thursday." This works just as well on "Shout out Wednesday," where colleagues can praise one another. Self-awareness is like any other muscle. It needs to be used to improve. It is also a great tool to use when creating plans for advancement.

What would you like to be more aware of? How would that affect the work you do?

"KNOWING OTHERS IS INTELLIGENCE. KNOWING YOURSELF IS TRUE WISDOM. MASTERING OTHERS IS STRENGTH. MASTERING YOURSELF IS TRUE POWER."

– LAO TZU –

#35

SERVICE

CONTRIBUTION TO THE WELFARE OF OTHERS.

Having a mindset of service is fundamental if you are looking to have a company that stands out from the rest. These days your Corporate Social Responsibility (CSR) rating is an aspect that new hires consider—and with good reason. People working with you want to be more than just a way for you to make money. Your customers and clients want you to care about who they are and the community they live in, not just the check they write to you. Prospering and engaging workplaces perform with a foundation of service to their employees, their customers, and their community.

Engage your employees to pick charities that have meaning to them, and set up how they can help. Have a food drive for the local food bank. Collect backpacks for kids going back to school. Plant flowers along a stretch of road. Spend time at a Boys and Girls Club. Create an opportunity for continuous service for the greater good. Educate and communicate the rewards of giving to the less fortunate.

How can you build a corporate identity that cares for the community outside your doors?

"EARN YOUR SUCCESS BASED ON SERVICE TO OTHERS, NOT AT THE EXPENSE OF OTHERS."

– H. JACKSON BROWN, JR. –

#36

SIMPLIFY

To diminish in scope or complexity.

We live in a complex world. Technology, although it promises to simplify your life, complicates it by giving you too many decisions to make. Find and focus on areas where you truly have the control to restructure and simplify. One person with too many deadlines can lead to poor performance and stress. Saving time, being more cost effective, and diminishing stress are all welcome attributes of finding simpler ways of doing work.

How do you simplify a workplace? When an organization gets too big for everyone to know each other one-on-one, and when you have remote offices and remote workers, it's time to be more strategic. Systemize processes to fend off duplication of information input. Have a purposeful method of assigning workloads. Find avenues of communication so that everyone gets the same vital information. This is a great way to stop rumors. Once started, gossip is very difficult to remedy.

What will happen when you choose to not complicate your life and the lives of your workforce?

"SIMPLIFYING YOUR LIFE AMPLIFIES YOUR FUTURE."

– **PHOENIX WHITE** –

#37

TRUST

THE RELIANCE ON THE INTEGRITY OF A PERSON OR ORGANIZATION.

You can't demand people trust you, or assume they will. If you do, you sound like the old-time cartoon of a car salesman: "Hey, trust me." It's phony and trite. Trust grows over time. It's built on a relationship with history. When you give trust, people are more prone to act trustworthy. In contrast, when you assume that people are not trustworthy, studies show that people tend to act accordingly. In other words your intention has influence on what you receive. Which do you want?

You wouldn't hire someone you don't trust, so give your employees the benefit of the doubt until proven otherwise. When situations arise that are outside of the "playbook," allow people the power to truly serve your clients and customers. No policy or procedure can cover every situation. Trust your workforce to come up with a solution that may be different than the "rule," but still within the framework of the company values. What a great way to keep customers too!

Will you be willing to trust enough to create greatness, or will you allow situations to go awry and diminish your goals?

"IF PEOPLE LIKE YOU, THEY'LL LISTEN TO YOU; BUT IF THEY TRUST YOU, THEY'LL DO BUSINESS WITH YOU."

– ZIG ZIGLAR –

WHAT DO YOU DO NOW?

Pick one concept. Work on that within your culture. Find ways to incorporate it in all aspects of your business. Give it time. Evaluate it. Tweak it. Make it work.

Need help? I can help you and your workplace achieve a higher level of expertise by incorporating any of these concepts into your existing culture. With each step you take, you will reap rewards for every person and your entire company. You pick what ideas are important to you today, because they will change, and we can work together to achieve the successes and goals you and your workforce deserve.

Contact Julie Ann Sullivan:
(724) 942-0486
JulieAnn@JulieAnnSullivan.com

Learn more:
WEBSITE: JulieAnnSullivan.com
TWITTER: JASatLNE
FACEBOOK: Julie Ann Sullivan Speaker